THE BRITISH MUSEUM
BIRDS

Proud Songsters

The thrushes sing as the sun is going,
And the finches whistle in ones and pairs,
And as it gets dark loud nightingales
In bushes
Pipe, as they can when April wears,
As if all Time were theirs.

These are brand-new birds of twelve months' growing,
Which a year ago, or less than twain,
No finches were, nor nightingales,
Nor thrushes,
But only particles of grain,
And earth, and air, and rain.

THOMAS HARDY (1840–1928)
England, winter 1927

THE BRITISH MUSEUM
BIRDS

EDITED BY
Mavis Pilbeam

THE BRITISH MUSEUM PRESS

In memory of my parents, who made birds and birdsong
a part of my everyday life.

I owe many thanks for all their help and advice to British Museum
colleagues Richard Blurton, Sheila Canby, Charlotte Cave, Marjorie Caygill,
Tim Clark and the Japanese Section, Lucinda Dean and Museum Assistants in
the Department of Asia, Mary Ginsberg, Sheila O'Connell, Richard Perfitt,
Jane Portal, Angela Roche and Museum Assistants in the Department of
Prints and Drawings, Axelle Russo and Nina Shandloff;
and also to Kate Down and Judith Chernaik.

© 2008 The Trustees of the British Museum

Mavis Pilbeam has asserted her moral right to be identified as the editor of this work

First published in 2008 by The British Museum Press
A division of The British Museum Company Ltd
38 Russell Square, London WC1B 3QQ
www.britishmuseum.co.uk

A catalogue record for this book is available from the British Library

ISBN 978-0-7141-5063-5

Poetry is reprinted by kind permission of the copyright holders (see pages 94–5).

Frontispiece: William de Morgan (1839–1917), *Ten Inch Birds*. Earthenware tile,
British, probably from the Merton Abbey period (1882–88).
Title page: Attributed to Hans Holbein the Younger (1497/8–1543), *Cock*. Detail from sheet
of drawings in pen and black ink on paper. From *The Jewellery Book*, German, 1532–43.
Page 96: Edouard Manet (1832–83), *Hirondelles* (swallows). Etching and drypoint,
illustration to the book *Le Fleuve* by Charles Cros, French, 1874.

Photography by the British Museum Department of Photography and Imaging
Designed and typeset in Centaur by Peter Ward
Printed in China by C&C Offset Printing Co., Ltd

INTRODUCTION

BIRDS are perhaps the most conspicuous and therefore the most familiar of all animals. Many species live in close proximity to humans, providing companionship with their endlessly active, often audible presence. Others, less bold, through their sheer secretiveness and beauty prompt us to go in search of them. All deserve our respect and care.

The British Museum's vast collections include images of birds from many parts of the world. Some are accurately detailed studies, others are more decorative, while yet others show birds going about their daily activities in natural settings, or may suggest a narrative. Some late nineteenth- and early twentieth-century artists such as Allen Seaby were strongly influenced by Japanese woodblock artists. Monochrome images can be as effective as colour, especially in depicting distinctive shapes and the fine texture of plumage, or suggesting lonely landscapes.

Each image is here paired with a poem. Poets have always been inspired by the variety and mystery of birds, their freedom of land, sea and sky, and their song – but also by their toughness, and their relation to people, often with thought-provoking or witty results.

Two contrasting poems about the blackbird's song complement Thomas Bewick's finely detailed watercolour print study. A sumptuous eighteenth-century Japanese hanging scroll depicts a white cockatoo which is described in imaginative detail in Mary Zoll's recent poem. The Somerset poet James Crowden's evocative lines on a working heron are echoed in Edward Detmold's powerful etching; Samuel Palmer's lone man with dog may well be humming a love song as he gazes on a skylark, while a sixteenth-century Safavid Iranian painting perfectly illustrates Thom Gunn's profound 'Tamer and Hawk'. John Clare, the epitome of the English bird poet, naturally appears several times. He is unexpectedly linked with an affectionate seventeenth-century Indian portrait of a hen and chicks, while Eric Daglish's quiet wood engraving surely *is* Clare's 'Early Nightingale'.

Grandeur, mystery, homeliness and what W. H. Davies called 'the beauty at my door' – these are so often missed, but this small book includes them all.

The Song

When Dasies pied, and Violets blew,
And Cuckow-buds of yellow hew:
And Ladie-smockes all silver white,
Do paint the Medowes with delight.
The Cuckow then on everie tree,
Mockes married men, for thus sings he,
Cuckow.
Cuckow, Cuckow: O word of feare,
Unpleasing to a married eare.

When Shepheards pipe on Oaten straws,
And merrie Larkes are Ploughmens clockes:
When Turtles tread, and Rookes and Dawes,
And Maidens bleach their summer smockes:
The Cuckow then on everie tree,
Mockes married men; for thus sings he,
Cuckow.
Cuckow, Cuckow: O word of feare,
Unpleasing to a married eare.

WILLIAM SHAKESPEARE (1564–1616)
England, from *Loves Labour's Lost*, 1598

The spelling of the First Folio (1623) has been retained.
Turtles are turtledoves; dawes are jackdaws.

Katsushika Hokusai (1760–1849), *Cuckoo and Azaleas*.
Woodblock print on paper, Japanese, *c.* 1828.

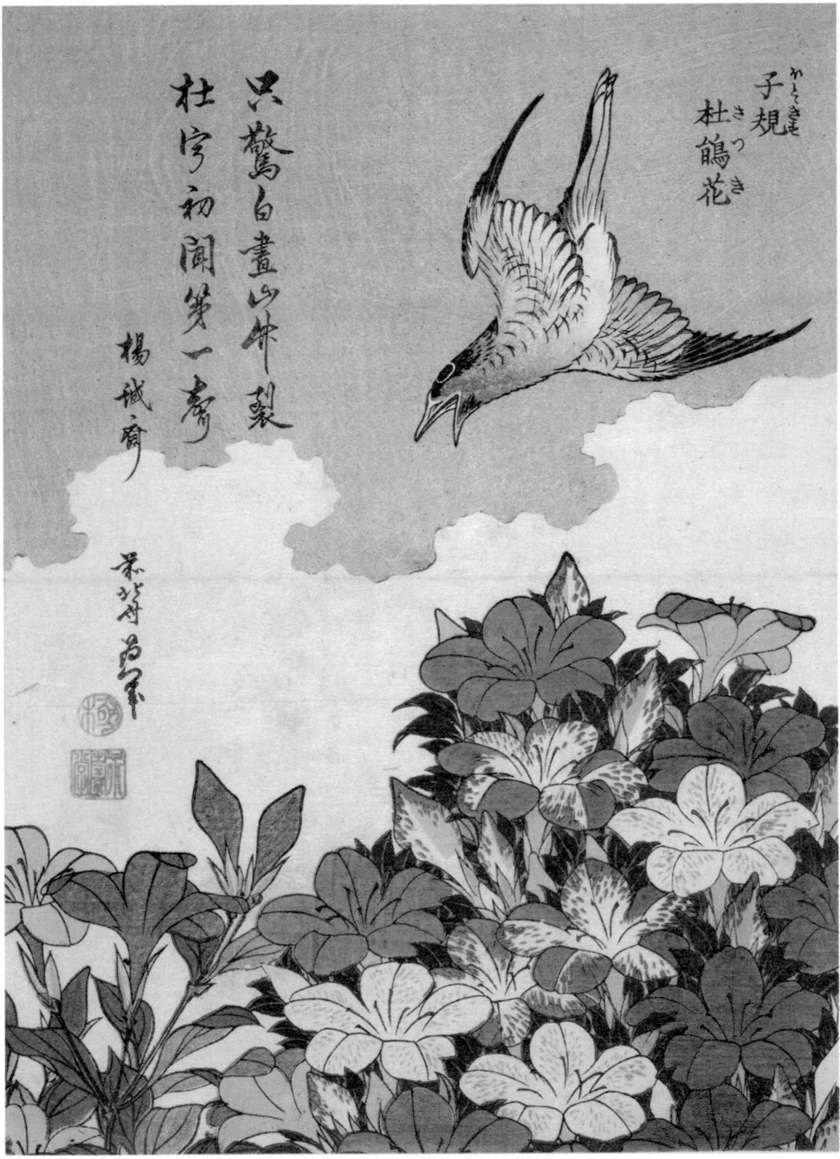
子規
杜鵑花
只驚白晝山中裂
杜宇初聞第一聲
楊誠齋

Roundel

Now welcome Summer with thy sunne soft,
That hast this winter's weathers overshake,
And driven away the longe nightes black.

Saint Valentine, that art full high aloft,
Thus singen smalle fowles for thy sake:
Now welcome Summer with thy sunne soft,
That hast this winter's weathers overshake.

Well have they cause for to gladden oft,
Since each of them recovered hath his make.
Full blissful may they singe when they wake:
Now welcome Summer with thy sunne soft,
That hast this winter's weathers overshake,
And driven away the longe nightes black!

GEOFFREY CHAUCER (*c.* 1343–1400)
England, from *The Parliament of Fowls* (*c.* 1382–3)

Make means mate.

Benjamin Green (1739–98), *Two Ring Doves on a Nest.*
Hand-coloured mezzotint, British, 1783–4.

A. Green pinx.   B. Green fecit.
London, Printed for & Sold by CARINGTON BOWLES, No 69 S.t Pauls Church Yard.
514   Published as the Act directs.

Two Pewits

Under the after-sunset sky
Two pewits sport and cry,
More white than is the moon on high
Riding the dark surge silently. Their cry
Is the one sound under the sky.
They alone move, now low, now high,
And merrily they cry
To the mischievous Spring sky,
Plunging earthward, tossing high,
Over the ghost who wonders why
So merrily they cry and fly,
Nor choose 'twixt earth and sky,
While the moon's quarter silently
Rides, and earth rests as silently.

EDWARD THOMAS (1878–1917)
England

The pewit or peewit is named after its call.
It is also known as the lapwing or green plover.
The poet describes the bird's unpredictable
tumbling flight.

Allen William Seaby (1867–1953), *Two Peewits*.
Colour woodcut on paper, British, early 20th century.

Birds' Nests

How fresh the air, the birds how busy now!
In every walk if I but peep I find
Nests newly made or finished all and lined
With hair and thistledown, and in the bough
Of little hawthorn, huddled up in green,
The leaves still thickening as the spring gets age,
The pink's, quite round and snug and closely laid,
And linnet's of materials loose and rough;
And still hedge-sparrow, moping in the shade
Near the hedge-bottom, weaves of homely stuff,
Dead grass and mosses green, an hermitage,
For secrecy and shelter rightly made;
And beautiful it is to walk beside
The lanes and hedges where their homes abide.

JOHN CLARE (1793–1864)
England

The pink or chaffinch is named after its call.

F. T. Baynes (active 1824–74), *Hedge Sparrow's Nest*.
Watercolour touched with bodycolour, strengthened with gum,
British, mid 19th century.

Home-Thoughts, from Abroad

Oh, to be in England
Now that April's there,
And whoever wakes in England
Sees, some morning, unaware,
That the lowest boughs and the brushwood sheaf
Round the elm-tree bole are in tiny leaf,
While the chaffinch sings on the orchard bough
In England—now!

II.

And after April, when May follows,
And the whitethroat builds, and all the swallows!
Hark, where my blossom'd pear-tree in the hedge
Leans to the field and scatters on the clover
Blossoms and dewdrops—at the bent spray's edge—
That's the wise thrush; he sings each song twice over,
Lest you should think he never could recapture
The first fine careless rapture!
And though the fields look rough with hoary dew,
All will be gay when noontide wakes anew
The buttercups, the little children's dower
—Far brighter than this gaudy melon-flower!

ROBERT BROWNING (1812–89)
England

Thomas Bewick (1753–1828), *Chaffinch*.
Pen and black ink with watercolour over graphite on paper,
British, 1797.

The Darkling Thrush

I leant upon a coppice gate
    When Frost was spectre-gray,
And Winter's dregs made desolate
    The weakening eye of day.
The tangled bine-stems scored the sky
    Like strings of broken lyres,
And all mankind that haunted nigh
    Had sought their household fires.

The land's sharp features seemed to be
    The Century's corpse outleant,
His crypt the cloudy canopy,
    The wind his death-lament.
The ancient pulse of germ and birth
    Was shrunken hard and dry,
And every spirit upon earth
    Seemed fervourless as I.

At once a voice arose among
    The bleak twigs overhead
In a full-hearted evensong
    Of joy illimited;
An aged thrush, frail, gaunt, and small,
    In blast-beruffled plume,
Had chosen thus to fling his soul
    Upon the growing gloom.

So little cause for carolings
    Of such ecstatic sound
Was written on terrestrial things
    Afar or nigh around,

Marie Littledale (b. 1910), 'T' – *Thrush* (song thrush).
Wood-engraved illustration to *An Alphabet of British Birds*, British, *c.* 1936.

That I could think there trembled through
    His happy good-night air
Some blessed Hope, whereof he knew
    And I was unaware.

THOMAS HARDY (1840–1928)
England, 31 December 1900

If the Owl Calls Again

at dusk
from the island in the river,
and it's not too cold,

I'll wait for the moon
to rise,
then take wing and glide
to meet him.

We will not speak,
but hooded against the frost
soar above
the alder flats, searching
with tawny eyes.

And then we'll sit
in the shadowy spruce
and pick the bones
of careless mice,

while the long moon drifts
toward Asia
and the river mutters
in its icy bed.

And when the morning climbs
the limbs
we'll part without a sound,

fulfilled, floating
homeward as
the cold world awakens.

JOHN HAINES (b. 1924), USA

Huang Yongyu (b. 1924), *Auspicious and Inauspicious Owls*.
Ink and colours on paper,
Chinese, spring 1977.

19

Pigeons

On shallow slates the pigeons shift together,
Backing against a thin rain from the west
Blown across each sunk head and settled feather.
Huddling round the warm stack suits them best,
Till winter daylight weakens, and they grow
Hardly defined against the brickwork. Soon,
Light from a small intense lopsided moon
Shows them, black as their shadows, sleeping so.

PHILIP LARKIN (1922–85)
England, 27 December 1955

Henri Guérard (1846–97), *Two Pigeons*.
Woodcut printed on reddish-brown oriental paper,
French, late 19th century.

bois taillé   imprimé par l'auteur   M. Marois

Turkey Vulture

The bird of the blood
hangs from the sun
on a rack of bones.
It is never alone
when it rests with its shoulders hunched,
looking for an open wound
to receive its penitent head.

DAVID CHORLTON (b. 1948)
Austria/England/USA

Anon, *Young Vulture*.
Painting on paper, Indian, Company school, *c*. 1800.

The Hawk

On Sunday the hawk fell on Bigging
    And a chicken screamed
    Lost in its own little snowstorm.
And on Monday he fell on the moor
    And the Field Club
    Raised a hundred silent prisms.
And on Tuesday he fell on the hill
    And the happy lamb
    Never knew why the loud collie straddled him.
And on Wednesday he fell on a bush
    And the blackbird
    Laid by his little flute for the last time.
And on Thursday he fell on Cleat
    And peerie Tom's rabbit
    Swung in a single arc from shore to hill.
And on Friday he fell on a ditch
    But the rampant rat,
    That eye and that tooth, quenched his flame.
And on Saturday he fell on Bigging
    And Jock lowered his gun
    And nailed a small wing over the corn.

GEORGE MACKAY BROWN (1921–96)
Scotland

The poet spent most of his life in the Orkneys and refers
to local place-names. The hawk is probably a buzzard.

Leo Frank (1884–1956), *Buzzard in Mist*.
Colour woodcut in the Japanese manner on oriental paper,
Austrian, early 20th century.

Snow

In the gloom of whiteness,
In the great silence of snow,
A child was sighing
And bitterly saying: 'Oh,
They have killed a white bird up there on her nest,
The down is fluttering from her breast!'
And still it fell through that dusky brightness
On the child crying for the bird in the snow.

EDWARD THOMAS (1878–1917)
England

Oda Kaisen (1785–1862), *Egret on Willow in Snow*.
Hanging scroll painting, ink and colours on silk,
Japanese, 19th century.

The Blackbird of Belfast Lough

The small bird
let a chirp
from its beak:
  I heard
woodnotes, whin-
gold, sudden.
The Lagan
  blackbird!

ANON. (c. 8th–9th century)
Ireland, translated from the Gaelic by Seamus Heaney

Vespers

O blackbird, what a boy you are!
How you do go it!
Blowing your bugle to that one sweet star –
How you do blow it!
And does she hear you, blackbird boy, so far?
Or is it wasted breath?
'Good Lord, she is so bright
Tonight!'
The blackbird saith.

THOMAS EDWARD BROWN (1830–97)
England

28

Thomas Bewick (1753–1828), *Black Ousel* (blackbird).
Pen and black ink with watercolour over graphite on paper, British, 1797.
Bewick's childhood home can be seen in the background.

The Lark in the Clear Air

Dear thoughts are in my mind
And my soul soars enchanted,
As I hear the sweet lark sing
In the clear air of the day.
For a tender beaming smile
To my hope has been granted,
And tomorrow she shall hear
All my fond heart would say.

I shall tell her all my love,
All my soul's adoration;
And I think she will hear me
And will not say me nay.
It is this that fills my soul
With its joyous elation,
As I hear the sweet lark sing
In the clear air of the day.

SAMUEL FERGUSON (1810–86)
Ireland

These verses are usually sung
to a traditional Irish air.

Samuel Palmer (1805–81), *The Skylark*.
Etching on chine appliqué, British, 1850.

Magpies

I have an orchard near my house
    Where poppies spread and corn has grown;
It is a holy place for weeds,
    Where seeds stay on and flower, till blown.
Into this orchard, wild and quiet,
    The Magpie comes, the Owl and Rook:
To see one Magpie is not well,
    But seeing two brings all good luck.
If Magpies think the same, and say,
    'Two humans bring good luck, not one' –
How they must cheer us, Love, together,
    And tremble when I come alone!

W. H. DAVIES (1871–1940)
England

Ding Liangxian (active late 17th century),
Magpies and Plum Tree.
Colour woodcut on paper,
Chinese, early Qing dynasty.

喜上眉稍

姑蘇丁亮先製

33

The Twa Corbies

As I was walking all alane,
I heard twa corbies making a mane;
The tane unto the t'other say,
'Where sall we gang and dine to-day?'

'In behint yon auld fail dyke,
I wot there lies a new slain knight;
And nae body kens that he lies there,
But his hawk, his hound, and lady fair.

'His hound is to the hunting gane,
His hawk to fetch the wild-fowl hame,
His lady's ta'en another mate,
Sae we may mak our dinner sweet.

'Ye'll sit on his white hause bane,
And I'll pike out his bonny blue een:
Wi' ae lock o' his gowden hair
We'll theek our nest when it grows bare.

'Mony a one for him makes mane,
But nane sall ken whare he is gane;
O'er his white banes, when they are bare,
The wind sall blaw for evermair.'

ANON. (before 1800)
Scotland, collected in *Minstrelsy of the Scottish Borders* (1803)
by Sir Walter Scott (1771–1832)

Corbie can refer to a crow or raven. Mane means moan;
fail: turf; hause bane: neck bone; theek: thatch.

Frank W. Benson (1862–1951), *Two Crows*.
Drypoint on Japanese paper, American, 1920.

Jenny Wren

Her sight is short, she comes quite near;
A foot to me's a mile to her;
And she is known as Jenny Wren,
The smallest bird in England. When
I heard that little bird at first,
Methought her frame would surely burst
With earnest song. Oft had I seen
Her running under leaves so green,
Or in the grass when fresh and wet,
As though her wings she would forget.
And, seeing this, I said to her –
'My pretty runner, you prefer
To be a thing to run unheard
Through leaves and grass, and not a bird!'
'Twas then she burst, to prove me wrong,
Into a sudden storm of song;
So very loud and earnest, I
Feared she would break her heart and die.
'Nay, nay,' I laughed, 'be you no thing
To run unheard, sweet scold, but sing!
O I could hear your voice near me,
Above the din in that oak tree,
When almost all the twigs on top
Had starlings chattering without stop.'

W. H. Davies (1871–1940)
England

The Wren

The wren
Looking here, looking there, —
'Dropped something?'

Issa Kobayashi (1763–1828)
Japan, translated from the Japanese by R. H. Blyth

Kitagawa Utamaro (*c.* 1754–1806), *Wren.*
Detail from woodblock-printed book, *Momo chidori kyōka awase*
(Myriad Birds: A Verse Competition), Japanese, *c.* 1790.

Lilac

Early morning the lilac
quivered, threw out a track
of fragrance to the street,
pervasive, watery-sweet.

The choreography of water,
the drift of scent caught at,
swirling away, blown back,
was the cunning of the lilac.

She bristled sweetness, arched
like a girl. A bullfinch perched
on her crown, immaculate
in his feathers. His weight

bothered the lilac, she bent
a little, her small tent
of pleasure collapsing
inward with the swaying.

GEORGE SZIRTES (b. 1948)
Hungary/England, from *Lilac, Laylock*

Allen William Seaby (1867–1953), *Two Bullfinches*.
Colour woodcut, British, early 20th century.

Pelicans

Four pelicans went over the house,
Sculled their worn oars over the courtyard: I saw that ungainliness
Magnifies the idea of strength.
A lifting gale of sea-gulls followed them; slim yachts of the element,
Natural growths of the sky, no wonder
Light wings to leave sea; but those grave weights toil, and are powerful,
And the wings torn with old storms to remember
The cone that the oldest redwood dropped from, the tilting of continents,
The dinosaur's day, the lift of new sea-lines.
The omnisecular spirit keeps the old with the new also.
Nothing at all has suffered erasure.
There is life not of our time. He calls ungainly bodies
As beautiful as the grace of horses.
He is weary of nothing; he watches air-planes; he watches pelicans.

ROBINSON JEFFERS (1887–1962)
USA

Frank W. Benson (1862–1951), *Perching Pelican*.
Etching on Japanese paper, American, 1915.

Just as this Island Belongs to the Gulls

Just as this island belongs to the gulls,
And the gulls to their cry
And their cry to the wind
And the wind to no one,

So is this islands the gulls,
And the gulls are their cry
And their cry is the wind
and the wind no one's.

HERMAN DE CONINCK (1944–97)
Belgium, translated from the Flemish by
Laure-Anne Bosselaar and Kurt Brown

Hans Frank (1884–1948), *Seagulls*.
Colour woodblock on oriental paper, Austrian, 1924.

Among Goldfinches

I am floating in a thin cloud
of them — simultaneous with
their soft whistles and rhythmic,
undulating flight — their tiny bodies
suspended just next to my ears
and shoulders, as we inhabit
each other's space and speed
and direction for a dozen wingbeats
and easy pedal strokes,
coasting on the morning wind.

Then they bank off, settle,
and sit like bright blossoms
in scrubby trail-side locusts, watching
my ordinary bicycle plunge ahead
into a canyon of Queen Anne's lace.

Later, as I struggle home against
the wind, their ghosts are glazing
my arms like dew and wrapping
the street full of traffic and starlings
in a yellow nimbus, dropping
an airy twitter and flutter of wings
onto the rolling earth, then drifting off
with a shy glance — feathered spirits
teasing like a voice that whispers:
Some riders here still believe in angels.

BILL MORGAN (b. 1940)
USA
This poem is about American goldfinches.
Queen Anne's lace is better known as cow parsley in Britain.

Nicolas Robert (1614–85),
detail from *American Goldfinch*.
Watercolour and bodycolour
on vellum, French, 17th century.

Pablo Picasso (1881–1973), *Le Chardonneret* (*The Goldfinch*).
Aquatint with scraper and drypoint, from '*Picasso: Eaux-fortes
originales pour les textes de Buffon*', French, 1936.

The Fern Owl's Nest

The weary woodman, rocking home beneath
His tightly banded faggot, wonders oft,
While crossing over the furze-crowded heath,
To hear the fern owl's cry, that whews aloft
In circling whirls, and often by his head
Whizzes as quick as thought and ill at rest,
As through the rustling ling with heavy tread
He goes, nor heeds he tramples near its nest,
That underneath the furze or squatting thorn
Lies hidden on the ground; and teasing round
That lonely spot, she wakes her jarring noise
To the unheeding waste, till mottled morn
Fills the red east with daylight's coming sound
And the heath's echoes mock the herding boys.

JOHN CLARE (1793–1864)
England

The fern owl is more commonly known as the nightjar.
The 'jarring noise' of its call can be heard at dusk and
dawn on heathland. It flies high and catches moths in
its hugely gaping bill, which has stiff bristles to net its
prey or protect its eyes from harm.

Peter Paillou (active 1763–1806), *Nightjar*.
Drawing on paper, bodycolour heightened with white,
British, late 18th century.

47

A Manifestation

unashamedly eccentric Joan
came for Thanksgiving
a bird on her shoulder —
an umbrella cockatoo six months old and
unimaginably white

this white is not an innocent velvet lily white
a tender sea-foam white
or a gentle melting-snowflake white

this is not a pristine isolated iceberg white
a momentary dream-fragment white
or a dangerous deep-pile polar-bear white

this is not a cold starlight-filtered-through-space white

this is a staggering white
hypnotic white
warm-blooded
feathered
phenomenal
multitudes of living white

the working
interconnected white
of her main flight feathers

the soft stunning white
of the silken down
on her chest

the personal white under her wings
where she invites scratching
occasionally

the fluffy puffed-cloud
almost frivolous white
of her ruff

the delicate white of the miniature cheek
     feathers
she angles forward
to close off the sides of her beak

the glowing white
of the expanding sideburns and crown
she raises for show

a crest more intricate than a Victorian-lace
     collar

more spectacular than a satin papal tiara

more wondrous than the halo of an angel

this
is god white

MARY ZOLL (b. 1947)
USA, November 1995

Masuyama Sessai (1755–1820),
detail from *Cockatoo and Mynah Bird*. Hanging scroll
painting, ink and colours on silk, Japanese, 1791.

Flamingo Watching

Wherever the flamingo goes,
she brings a city's worth
of furbelows. She seems
unnatural by nature —
too vivid and peculiar
a structure to be pretty,
and flexible to the point
of oddity. Perched on
those legs, anything she does
seems like an act. Descending
on her egg or draping her head
along her back, she's
too exact and sinuous
to convince an audience
she's serious. The natural elect,
they think, would be less pink,
less able to relax their necks,
less flamboyant in general.
They privately expect that it's some
poorly jointed bland grey animal
with mitts for hands
whom God protects.

KAY RYAN (b. 1945)
USA

John White (active 1570–90), *A Flamingo*.
Watercolour over black lead, touched with
bodycolour and white, British, *c.* 1585.

60

Washing Day

The cormorants
hang their feathers
out to dry –
black velvet rags
showing threadbare
in the wind.
Like old women
living in the past,
they tend their
tattered finery
with talon fingers
and black
remembering eyes.

RITA SUMMERS (active from 1986)
Australia (Tasmania)

Norbetine Von Bresslern-Roth (1891–1978), *Cormorants.*
Colour woodblock print in grey, brown, yellow and black,
Austrian, *c.* 1930.

From *The Seafarer*

There heard I naught but seething sea,
Ice-cold wave, awhile a song of swan.
There came to charm me gannets' pother
And whimbrels' trills for the laughter of men,
Kittiwake singing instead of mead.
Storms there the stacks thrashed, there answered them the tern
With icy feathers; full oft the erne wailed around
Spray-feathered . . .

ANON. (before *c.* 685), collected in *The Exeter Book, c.* 1000
England, translated from the Old English by James Fisher

Erne is a white-tailed sea eagle.

Fisher nominates the poet of *The Seafarer* as the first ever ornithologist
and suggests that he may have been describing the Bass Rock in the
Firth of Forth near Edinburgh, where many of the birds he mentions
can still be seen. It is now home to one of the largest gannet colonies
in the world, though Place does not show this bird in his etching.

Francis Place (1647–1728), *The Bass Island*.
Etching from *Set of Birds Dedicated to Lord Maitland*, British, 1686.

Riddle

When it is earth I tread, make tracks upon water
or keep the houses, hushed is my clothing,
clothing that can hoist me above house-ridges
at times toss me into the tall heaven
where the strong cloud-wind carries me on
over cities and countries; accoutrements that
throb out sound, thrilling strokes
deep-soughing song, as I sail alone
over field and flood, faring on,
resting nowhere. My name is . . .

ANON. (*c.* early 8th century), collected in *The Exeter Book*, *c.* 1000
England, translated from the Old English by Michael Alexander

The Silver Swan

The silver Swan, who living had no Note,
When death approached unlocked her silent throat,
Leaning her breast against the reedy shore,
Thus sung her first and last, and sung no more:
'Farewell all joys, O death come close mine eyes,
More Geese than Swans now live, more fools than wise.'

ANON., *c.* 1600
England

It has been suggested that this poem may refer to the death in 1599 of
Edmund Spenser, Poet Laureate and author of the epic poem *The Færie
Queene*. It was set to music by Orlando Gibbons in his *First Set of Madrigals
and Motets*, 1612.

Allen William Seaby (1867–1953), *Swans*.
Colour woodcut on paper, British, early 20th century.

Heron Fishing — Heron Rising

Silent and stealthy sleek   steely still, beady eyed
Narrow neck craned and tufted   the dapper dandy
Poised above the ripple   hidden in the reeds
Vain admirer of his own reflection   lurks like sculpture
Sly sentinel   monocled hunchback
About to move   fleet and stabbing
The sharp punishing blade   darts
Fractures the water   pinions its prey
Swift purpose   gulps and gulps again . . .

Grey merging with sky . . .   swallows silver on the green bank

Long and lanky, the Fisher King   legs it like a stork
Undercarriage trailing   ungainly, gawky
Hefty wings massage the air   as it rises up
As if casually, patrols   its kingdom
Back alleys and damp waterways   ditches interlaced
The shamanic realm   sky and water
Slowly sauntering seawards   bends of sluggish rivers
Slippery and slimy   oozey eel-laden mud
Half hidden in tidal sludge   surfaces from the depths
The dark low, slow flow   of the soft, flat, fat, land
Still wriggling within the belly   last in flight meal.

JAMES CROWDEN (b. 1954)
England

Edward Julius Detmold (1883–1957), *Off to the Fishing Grounds*.
Etching printed in brown ink, British, 1899.

Wagtail and Baby

A baby watched a ford, whereto
    A wagtail came for drinking;
A blaring bull went wading through,
    The wagtail showed no shrinking.

A stallion splashed his way across,
    The birdie nearly sinking;
He gave his plumes a twitch and toss,
    And held his own unblinking.

Next saw the baby round the spot
    A mongrel slowly slinking;
The wagtail gazed, but faltered not
    In dip and sip and prinking.

A perfect gentleman then neared;
    The wagtail, in a winking,
With terror rose and disappeared;
    The baby fell a-thinking.

THOMAS HARDY (1840–1928)
England

Eric Fitch Daglish (1894–1966), *The Pied Wagtail*.
Wood engraving, British, *c.* 1926.

The Hoopoe

Dear hoopoe, welcome! You will be our guide;
It was on you King Solomon relied
To carry messages between
His court and distant Sheba's lovely queen.
He knew your language and you knew his heart —
As his close confidant you learnt the art
Of holding demons captive underground,
And for these valiant exploits you were crowned.

Farid ud-Din Attar (*c.* 1120), from *The Conference of the Birds*
Persia (Iran), translated from the Persian/Farsi by
Afkham Darbandi and Dick Davis

The Conference of the Birds is a poem about Sufism, the mystic form of Islam.
Under the direction of their leader, the hoopoe, the birds are searching for
the ideal spiritual king, the mythical *simorgh*. Their quest symbolizes the
mystic's yearning for annihilation in God, but the serious intent of the
poem is lightened with humour as the hoopoe tells a series of fables.

The hoopoe's role as Solomon's messenger to the Queen of Sheba is
described in the Qur'an, *sura* 27, verses 20–31.

John White (active 1570–90), *Common Hoopoe*.
Watercolour and bodycolour over black lead,
heightened with white, British, *c.* 1585.

Tamer and Hawk

I thought I was so tough,
But gentled at your hands,
Cannot be quick enough
To fly for you and show
That when I go I go
At your commands.

Even in flight above
                    I am no longer free:
You seeled me with your love,
I am blind to other birds —
The habit of your words
Has hooded me.

As formerly, I wheel
I hover and I twist,
But only want the feel,
In my possessive thought,
Of catcher and of caught
Upon your wrist.

You but half civilise,
Taming me in this way.
Through having only eyes
For you I fear to lose,
I lose to keep, and choose
Tamer as prey.

THOM GUNN (1929–2004)
England, from *Fighting Terms*, 1954

Anon., *Court Falconer with a Falcon on his Wrist*.
Painting in gouache and gold on paper,
Safavid Iran, Qazvin style, *c.* 1580.

From *The Swallow*

The gorse is yellow on the heath,
  The banks with speedwell flowers are gay,
The oaks are budding; and beneath,
The hawthorn soon will bear the wreath,
  The silver wreath of May.
The welcome guest of settled Spring,
  The swallow too has come at last;
Just at sun-set, when thrushes sing,
I saw her dash with rapid wing,
  And hail'd her as she pass'd.
Come, summer visitant, attach
  To my reed roof your nest of clay,
And let my ear your music catch
Low twittering underneath the thatch
  At the gray dawn of day.

CHARLOTTE SMITH (1749–1806)
England

Frederick Walker (1840–75), *The First Swallow*.
Watercolour and bodycolour on paper,
British, mid 19th century.
As part of his apprenticeship in the mid 1850s, like
many artists of his time, Walker drew objects in the
British Museum, especially the Elgin Marbles.

A bush warbler comes:
   all muddy are the feet he wipes
     upon the blooming plums.

Issa Kobayashi (1763–1828)
Japan, translated from the Japanese
by Harold G. Henderson

Bush warbler –
   A dropping on the rice cake
    At the verandah's edge.

Matsuo Bashō (1644–94)
Japan, translated from the Japanese
by Makoto Ueda

In Japan the bush warbler arrives with the early-flowering
plum blossom and is an eagerly awaited harbinger of spring,
like the cuckoo in England.

Niwa Tōkei (1760–1822?), *Bush Warbler*.
Woodblock *surimono* (limited edition) print,
Japanese, early 19th century.

O Dreams, O Destinations (9)

To travel like a bird, lightly to view
Deserts where stone gods founder in the sand,
Ocean embraced in a white sleep with land;
To escape time, always to start anew.
To settle like a bird, make one devoted
Gesture of permanence upon the spray
Of shaken stars and autumns: in a bay
Beyond the crestfallen surges to have floated.
Each is our wish. Alas, the bird flies blind,
Hooded by a dark sense of destination;
Her weight on the glass calm leaves no impression,
Her home is soon a basketful of wind.
Travellers, we're fabric of the road we go;
We settle, but like feathers on time's flow.

C. DAY LEWIS (1904–72)
England

The Canada geese which breed in Canada migrate south in
the autumn and return in the spring along flyways following
various routes: the Atlantic coast, the Mississippi River, the
Rocky Mountains and the Pacific seaboard.

Frank W. Benson (1862–1951), *Migrating Geese*.
Etching on Japanese paper, American, 1916.

The Eagle

He clasps the crag with crookèd hands;
Close to the sun in lonely lands,
Ringed with the azure world he stands.

The wrinkled sea beneath him crawls;
He watches from his mountain walls,
And like a thunderbolt he falls.

ALFRED, LORD TENNYSON (1809–92)
England

While in the Lake District in the summer of 1850,
Tennyson entered this poem, published a year later,
in Dorothy Wordsworth's album.

Gan Tai (1782–1865), *Eagle and Monkey*.
Hanging scroll painting, ink and colours on paper,
Japanese, 1838.

The Kingfisher

It was the Rainbow gave thee birth,
    And left thee all her lovely hues;
And, as her mother's name was Tears,
    So runs it in thy blood to choose
For haunts the lonely pools, and keep
In company with trees that weep.

Go you and, with such glorious hues,
    Live with proud Peacocks in green parks;
On lawns as smooth as shining glass,
    Let every feather show its marks;
Get thee on boughs and clap thy wings
Before the windows of proud kings.

Nay, lovely Bird, thou art not vain;
    Thou hast no proud, ambitious mind;
I also love a quiet place
    That's green, away from all mankind;
A lonely pool, and let a tree
Sigh with her bosom over me.

W. H. DAVIES (1871–1940)
England, from *Farewell to Poesy*, 1910

Allen William Seaby (1867–1953), *Kingfisher*.
Colour woodcut on paper, British, early 20th century.

I saw a Peacock with a Fiery Tail

I saw a Peacock with a fiery tail
I saw a blazing Comet drop down hail
I saw a Cloud with Ivy circled round
I saw a sturdy Oak creep on the ground
I saw a Pismire swallow up a Whale
I saw a raging Sea brim full of Ale
I saw a Venice Glass sixteen foot deep
I saw a Well full of men's tears that weep
I saw their Eyes all in a flame of fire
I saw a House as big as the Moon and higher
I saw the Sun even in the midst of night
I saw the Man that saw this wondrous sight.

Anon. (17th century)
England

The editor (1671) writes: 'These following are to be
understood two ways', and inserts a comma in the
middle of all but the last line.

This poem and image both refer to the elements and other natural
phenomena. Shravana is the month of monsoons, which bring
heavy rainfall and lightning.

Anon., *The month of Shravana* (July/August),
detail of a leaf from a dispersed *barahmasa* (song of the seasons).
Painting in gouache on paper, Bundi, West India, late 17th century.

Proud Maisie

Proud Maisie is in the wood,
    Walking so early;
Sweet robin sits on the bush,
    Singing so rarely.

'Tell me, thou bonny bird,
    When shall I marry me?'
'When six braw gentlemen
    Kirkward shall carry ye.'

'Who makes the bridal bed,
    Birdie, say truly?'
'The grey-headed sexton
    That delves the grave duly.

'The glow-worm o'er grave and stone
    Shall light thee steady.
The owl from the steeple sing
    "Welcome, proud lady."'

SIR WALTER SCOTT (1771–1832)
Scotland

In Scott's novel *The Heart of Midlothian* (1818), the madwoman
Madge Wildfire, crazed by seduction and the murder of her
infant, sings these words on her deathbed.

Thomas Bewick (1753–1828), *Robin Redbreast*.
Pen and black ink with watercolour
over graphite on paper, British, 1797.

Sounds in the Wood

Trees breathe
Quiet in the wood.
Winds hush
Cradled in the branches.
Jays squall
Carping in the startled tree-tops.
Tits pipe
Keen in the secret, the secret thicket.

Mavis Pilbeam (b. 1946)
England, October 2006, near Thorncombe, Dorset

William Giles (1872–1939), *The Haunt of the Jay*.
Colour woodcut on paper, British, *c.* 1932.

To Sparrows Fighting

Stop, feathered bullies!
    Peace, angry birds;
You common Sparrows that,
    For a few words,
Roll fighting in wet mud,
To shed each other's blood.

Look at those Linnets, they
    Like ladies sing;
See how those Swallows, too,
    Play on the wing;
All other birds close by
Are gentle, clean and shy.

And yet maybe your life's
    As sweet as theirs;
The common poor that fight
    Live not for years
In one long frozen state
Of anger, like the great.

W. H. Davies (1871–1940)
England, from *Songs of Joy*, 1911

This poem is about house sparrows,
while the image shows tree sparrows
with their chestnut-coloured heads.

Anon., *Sparrows and Wisteria*.
Fan painting, ink and colours on silk,
Chinese, early Qing dynasty, 17th century.

Early Nightingale

When first we hear the shy-come nightingales,
They seem to mutter o'er their songs in fear,
And, climb we e'er so soft the spinney rails,
All stops as if no bird was anywhere.
The kindled bushes with the young leaves thin
Let curious eyes to search a long way in,
Until impatience cannot see or hear
The hidden music; gets but little way
Upon the path — when up the songs begin,
Full loud a moment and then low again.
But when a day or two confirms her stay
Boldly she sings and loud for half the day;
And soon the village brings the woodman's tale
Of having heard the new-come nightingale.

JOHN CLARE (1793–1864)
England

Eric Fitch Daglish (1894–1966), *The Nightingale*.
Wood engraving, British, *c.* 1930.

The Nightingale   Eric Daglish

Quail's Nest

I wandered out one rainy day
    And heard a bird with merry joys
Cry 'wet my foot' for half the way;
    I stood and wondered at the noise,

When from my foot a bird did flee –
    The rain flew bouncing from her breast –
I wondered what the bird could be,
    And almost trampled on her nest.

The nest was full of eggs and round;
    I met a shepherd in the vales,
And stood to tell him what I found.
    He knew and said it was a quail's,

For he himself the nest had found,
    Among the wheat and on the green,
When going on his daily round,
    With eggs as many as fifteen.

Among the stranger birds they feed,
    Their summer flight is short and low;
There's very few know where they breed,
    And scarcely any where they go.

JOHN CLARE (1793–1864)
England

'Wet my foot' is a popular rendering of the call
of the cock quail.

竹
鶏

Kitao Masayoshi (1764–1824), *Quail with Blue Flowers*.
From *Raikin zui* (Picture Collection of Imported Birds),
woodblock-printed book, Japanese, *c*. 1790.

Pied Beauty

Glory be to god for dappled things —
    For skies of couple-colour as a brinded cow;
        For rose-moles all in stipple upon trout that swim;
Fresh-firecoal chestnut-falls; finches wings;
    Landscape plotted and pieced — fold, fallow, and plough;
        And áll trádes, their gear and tackle and trim.

All things counter, original, spare, strange;
    Whatever is fickle, freckled (who knows how?)
        With swift, slow; sweet, sour; adazzle, dim;
He fathers-forth whose beauty is past change:
                        Praise him.

GERARD MANLEY HOPKINS (1844–89)
England, summer 1877

Noda Tōmin (active 1790s), *Pied Kingfisher*.
Painting, ink and colours on paper, Japanese, 1792.
Copied from Ogiwara Tōkitsu's copy of the original drawing
by Kanō Tan'yū (1602–74).

Hen's Nest

Among the orchard weeds, from every search,
Snugly and sure, the old hen's nest is made,
Who cackles every morning from her perch
To tell the servant girl new eggs are laid;
Who lays her washing by, and far and near
Goes seeking all about from day to day,
And stung with nettles tramples everywhere;
But still the cackling pullet lays away.
The boy on Sundays goes the stack to pull
In hopes to find her there, but naught is seen,
And takes his hat and thinks to find it full,
She's laid so long so many might have been.
But naught is found and all is given o'er
Till the young brood come chirping to the door.

JOHN CLARE (1793–1864)
England

Attributed to Mansur, Nadir al-'Asr, *A Hen and Chicks*.
Painting in gouache on cotton, India,
Mughal, early 17th century.

From *Ducks*

To F.M. who drew them in Holzminden Prison (*c.* 1916)

From troubles of the world
I turn to ducks,
Beautiful comical things
Sleeping or curled
Their heads beneath white wings
By water cool,
Or finding curious things
To eat in various mucks
Beneath the pool,
Tails uppermost, or waddling
Sailor-like on the shores
Of ponds, or paddling
– Left! Right! – with fanlike feet
Which are for steady oars
When they (white galleys) float
Each bird a boat
Rippling at will the sweet
Wide waterway . . .

FREDERICK WILLIAM HARVEY (1888–1957)
England

Katsushika Hokusai (1760–1849),
detail from *Ducks in a Stream*.
Hanging scroll painting, ink and
colours on silk, Japanese, 1847.

FURTHER READING AND SOURCES

Poetry reprinted by permission of the copyright holders (original page numbers in italic)

ALEXANDER, Michael (trans., ed.), *The Earliest English Poems*, Penguin Classics, London, 1966 (*p. 94*): © Michael Alexander 1966, 1977, 1991, by permission of Penguin Books Ltd

Anon., 'I Saw a Peacock', from *Westminster Drollery. Or, A Choice Collection of the Newest Songs & Poems both at Court and Theaters. By A Person of Quality*, London, 1671 (*p. 50*)

Anon., 'The Silver Swan', from *The Oxford Book of English Madrigals*, ed. Philip Ledger, Oxford University Press, London, 1978 (*p. 310*)

ATTAR, Farid ud-Din, trans. Afkham Darbandi and Dick Davis, *The Conference of the Birds*, Penguin Classics, London, 1984 (*p. 29*): © Afkham Darbandi and Dick Davis 1984, by permission of Penguin Books Ltd

BLYTH, R. H., *Haiku* (4 vols), Hokuseido, Tokyo, 1952 (vol. IV, Autumn–Winter, *p. 79*)

BROWN, George Mackay, *The Collected Poems of George Mackay Brown*, ed. Archie Bevan and Brian Murray, John Murray, London, 2005 (*p. 51*)

BROWN, Thomas Edward, *The Collected Poems of T. E. Brown*, with introduction by W. E. Henley, Macmillan & Co., London, 1900 (*p. 689*): © Manx Museum Trust 1976

BROWNING, Robert, *Browning, Poetical Works 1833–1864*, ed. Ian Jack, Oxford University Press, Oxford, 1970 (*p. 431*)

CHAUCER, Geoffrey, from *Poems on the Underground*, ed. Gerard Benson, Judith Chernaik and Cicely Herbert, Cassell Publishers, London, 1991, 7th edn 1998 (*p. 90*): by permission of Judith Chernaik

CHORLTON, David, *Sightings*, Palanquin Press, University of South Carolina, Aiken, 2000: by permission of the poet

CLARE, John, *The Poems of John Clare*, ed. with introduction by J. W. Tibble (2 vols), J. M. Dent & Sons, London, 1935 (*pp. 242, 247, 310, 339, 367*)

CONINCK, Herman de, *The Plural of Happiness: Selected Poems of Herman de Coninck*, trans. Laure-Anne Bosselaar and Kurt Brown, Oberlin College Press, Oberlin, OH, 2006 (*p. 57*): © 2006 Oberlin College Press

CROWDEN, James (poems) and WRIGHT, George (photographs), *In Time of Flood*, The Parrett Trail Partnership, Yeovil, Somerset, 1996 (*p. 49*): by permission of the poet

DAVIES, W. H., *Collected Poems of W. H. Davies*, with introduction by Osbert Sitwell, Jonathan Cape, London, 1942 (*pp. 99, 107, 150, 442*): © Mrs H. M. Davies Will Trust

FERGUSON, Samuel, *The Poems of Samuel Ferguson*, ed. Padraic Colum, Allen Figgis, Dublin, 1963 (*p. 90*)

FISHER, James, *The Shell Bird Book*, Ebury Press and Michael Joseph, London, 1966 (*p. 43*)

GUNN, Thom, *Thom Gunn: Collected Poems*, Faber and Faber, London, 1993 (*p. 29*)

HAINES, John, *The Owl in the Mask of the Dreamer: Collected Poems by John Haines*, Graywolf Press, St Paul, MN, 1996 (*p. 9*)

HARDY, Thomas, *The Complete Poems of Thomas Hardy*, ed. James Gibson, New Wessex edn, Macmillan & Co., London, 1978 (*pp. 119, 241, 816*)

HARVEY, F. W., *F. W. Harvey: Collected Poems (1912–1957)*, Douglas McLean, Coleford, 1983 (*p. 13*)

HEANEY, Seamus, *Preoccupations: Selected Prose 1968–1978*, Faber and Faber, London, 1980 (*p. 181*)

HENDERSON, Harold G., *An Introduction to Haiku*, Anchor Books, New York, 1958 (*p. 145*): © Harold G. Henderson 1958, by permission of Doubleday, a division of Random House, Inc.

HOPKINS, Gerard Manley, *The Poems of Gerard Manley Hopkins*, ed. W. H. Gardner and N. H. McKenzie, Oxford University Press, Oxford, 1918, 4th edn 1967 (*pp. 69–70*)

JEFFERS, Robinson, *The Collected Poetry of Robinson Jeffers*, vol. 1, Stanford University Press, Palo Alto, CA, 2001 (*p. 207*): © Jeffers Literary Properties, by permission of Stanford University Press, *www.sup.org*

LARKIN, Phillip, *Collected Poems*, ed. with introduction by Anthony Thwaite, Faber and Faber, London, 1988 (*p. 109*)

LEWIS, C. Day, *The Complete Poems of C. Day Lewis*, Sinclair-Stevenson, London, 1992 (*p. 321*)

MORGAN, Bill: by permission of the poet

PILBEAM, Mavis: by permission of the poet

RYAN, Kay, *Flamingo Watching*, Copper Beech Press, Brown University, Providence, RI, 1994 (*p. 9*): © Kay Ryan

SCOTT, Sir Walter, *The Poetical Works of Sir Walter Scott*, ed. J. Logie Robertson, Oxford University Press, London, 1904, 1947 (*p. 774*)

SHAKESPEARE, William, *The Complete Works of William Shakespeare*, vol. 1, *Comedies*, The Nonesuch Press, London, 1953 (*p. 540*)

SMITH, Charlotte, *Beachy Head with Other Poems*, J. Johnson, St Paul's Churchyard, London, 1807 (*p. 79*)

SUMMERS, Rita (*http://incolor.inebraska.com/tgannon/bird.html*)

SZIRTES, George, *Collected Poems*, Bloodaxe Books, Tarset, Northumberland, 2008: by permission of Bloodaxe Books

TENNYSON, Alfred, Lord, *Juvenilia and English Idylls*, Macmillan & Co., London, 1906 (*p. 268*)

THOMAS, Edward, *Collected Poems: Edward Thomas*, Faber and Faber, London, 1936 (*pp. 24, 171*)

UEDA Makoto, *Bashō and His Interpreters: Selected Hokku with commentary*, Stanford University Press, Stanford, CA, 1992 (*p. 336*): © Board of Trustees of the Leland Stanford Jr University 1992, by permission of Stanford University Press, *www.sup.org*

ZOLL, Mary: by permission of the poet

ILLUSTRATION REFERENCES

Photography © The Trustees of the British Museum, courtesy Department of Photography and Imaging